SNAKE

Coloring Book for Kids Ages 4-8

by Nick Marshall

This Coloring Book Belongs to

____

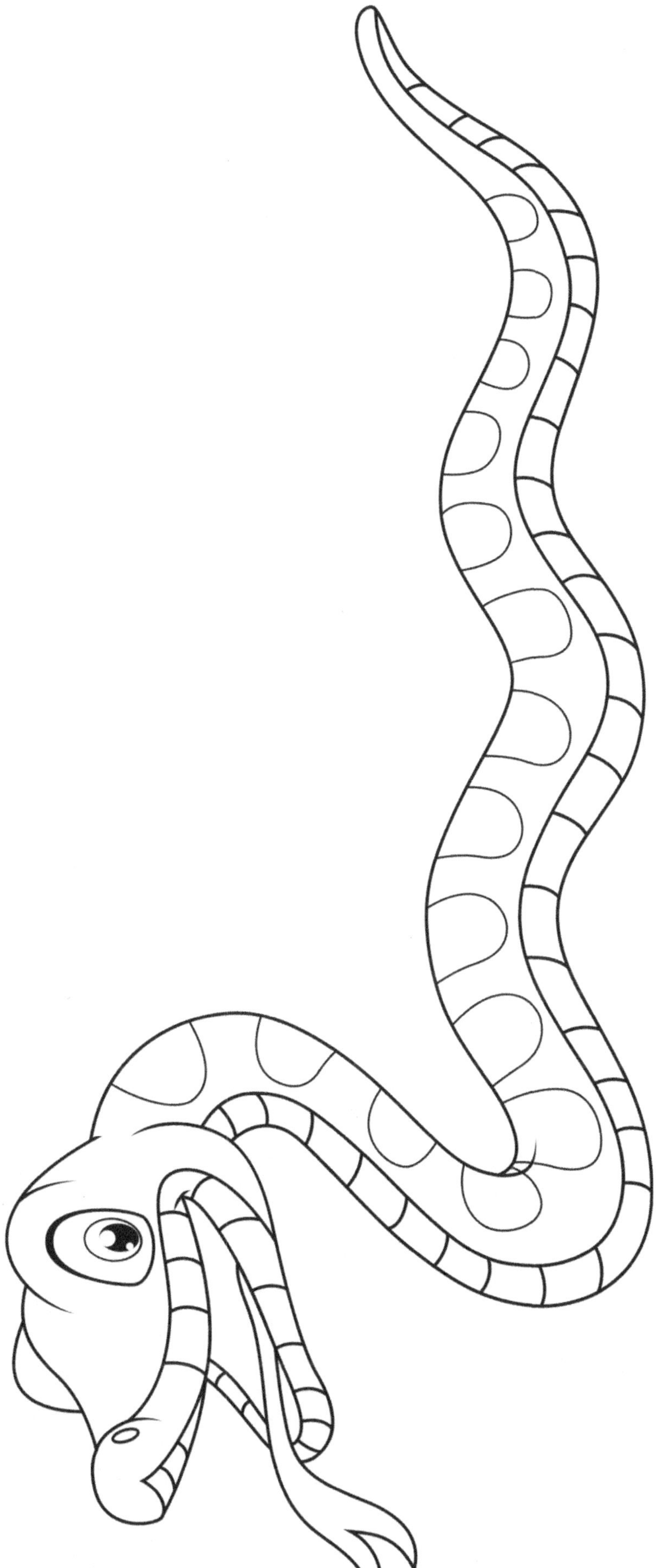

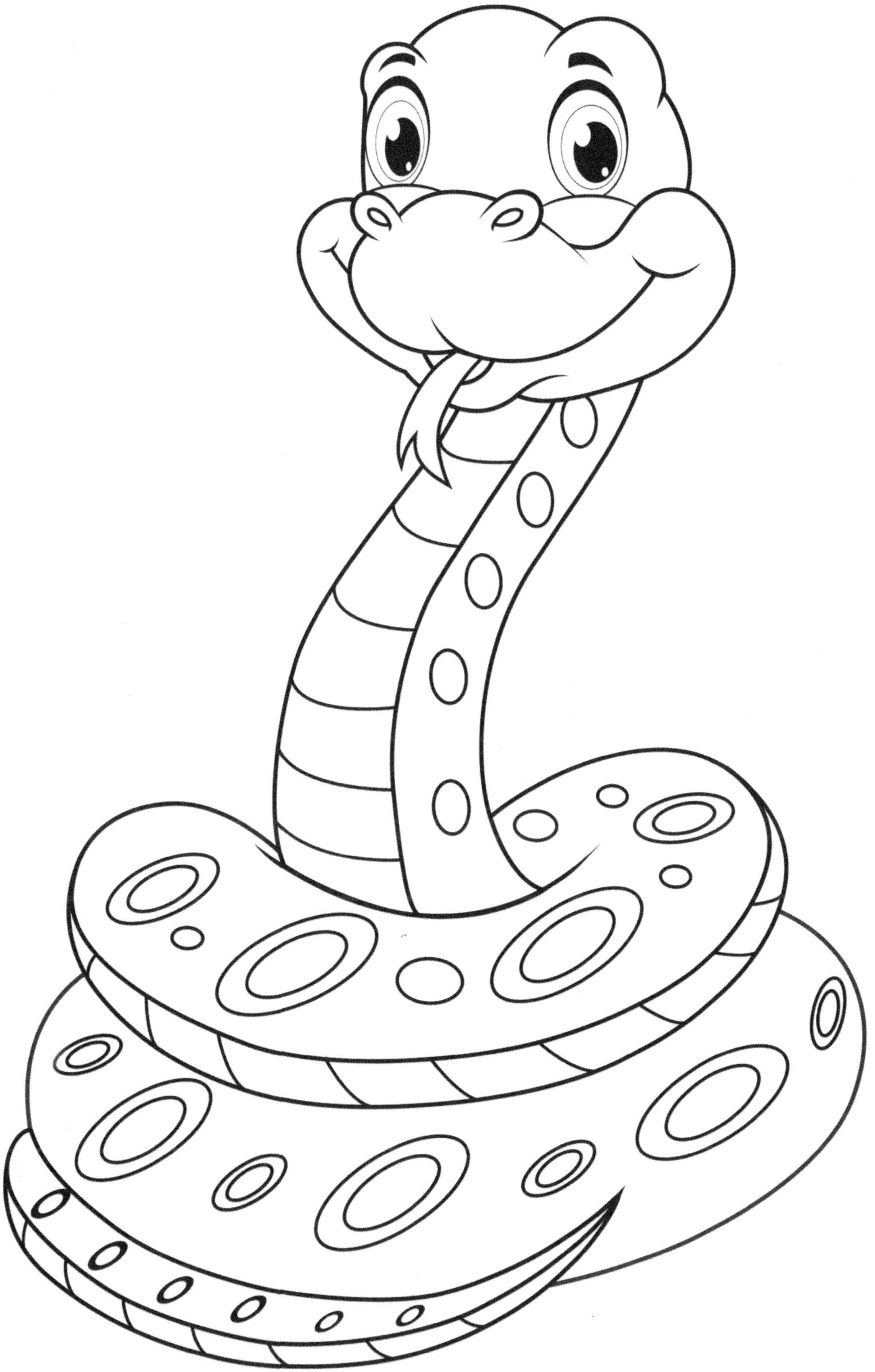

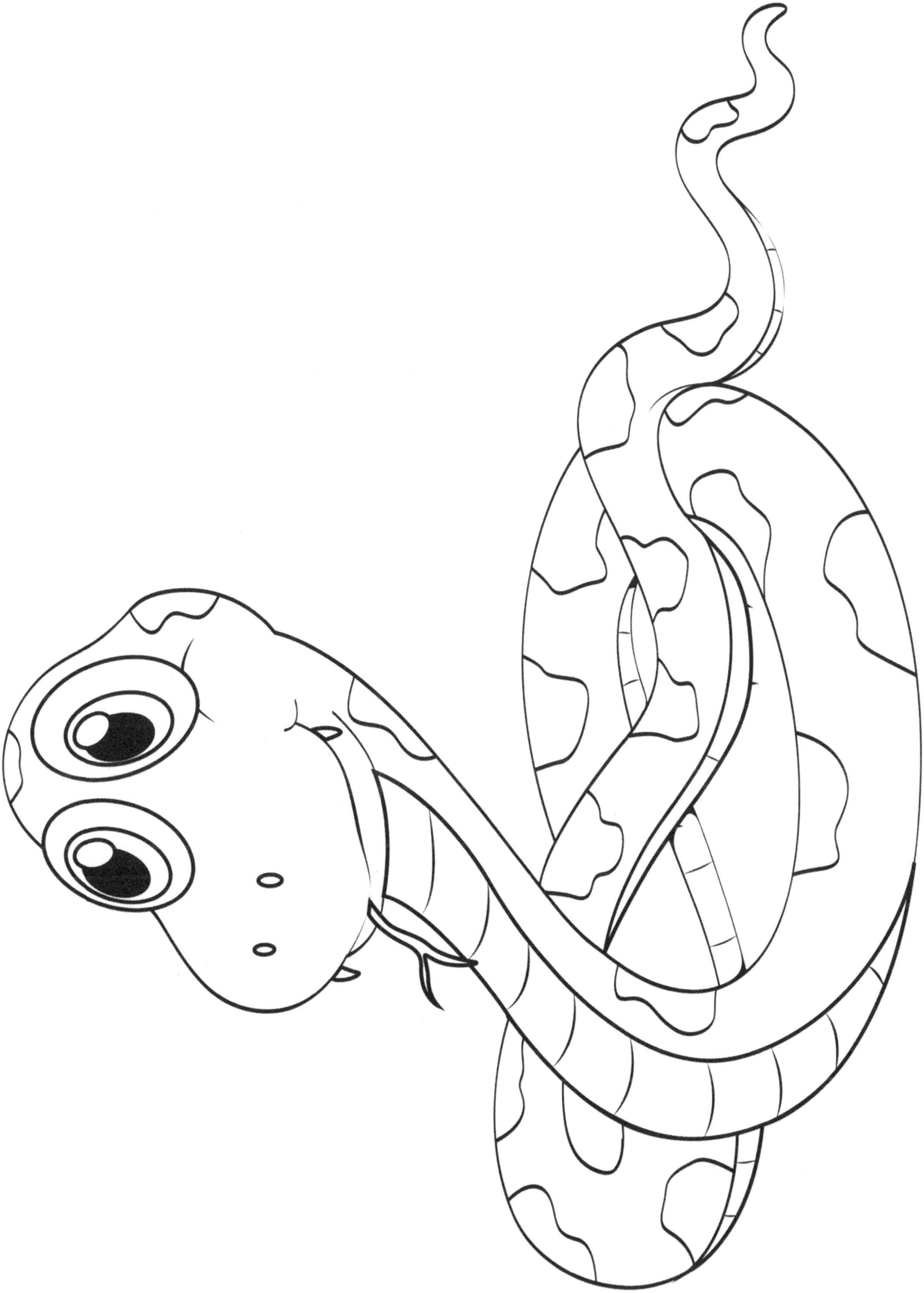

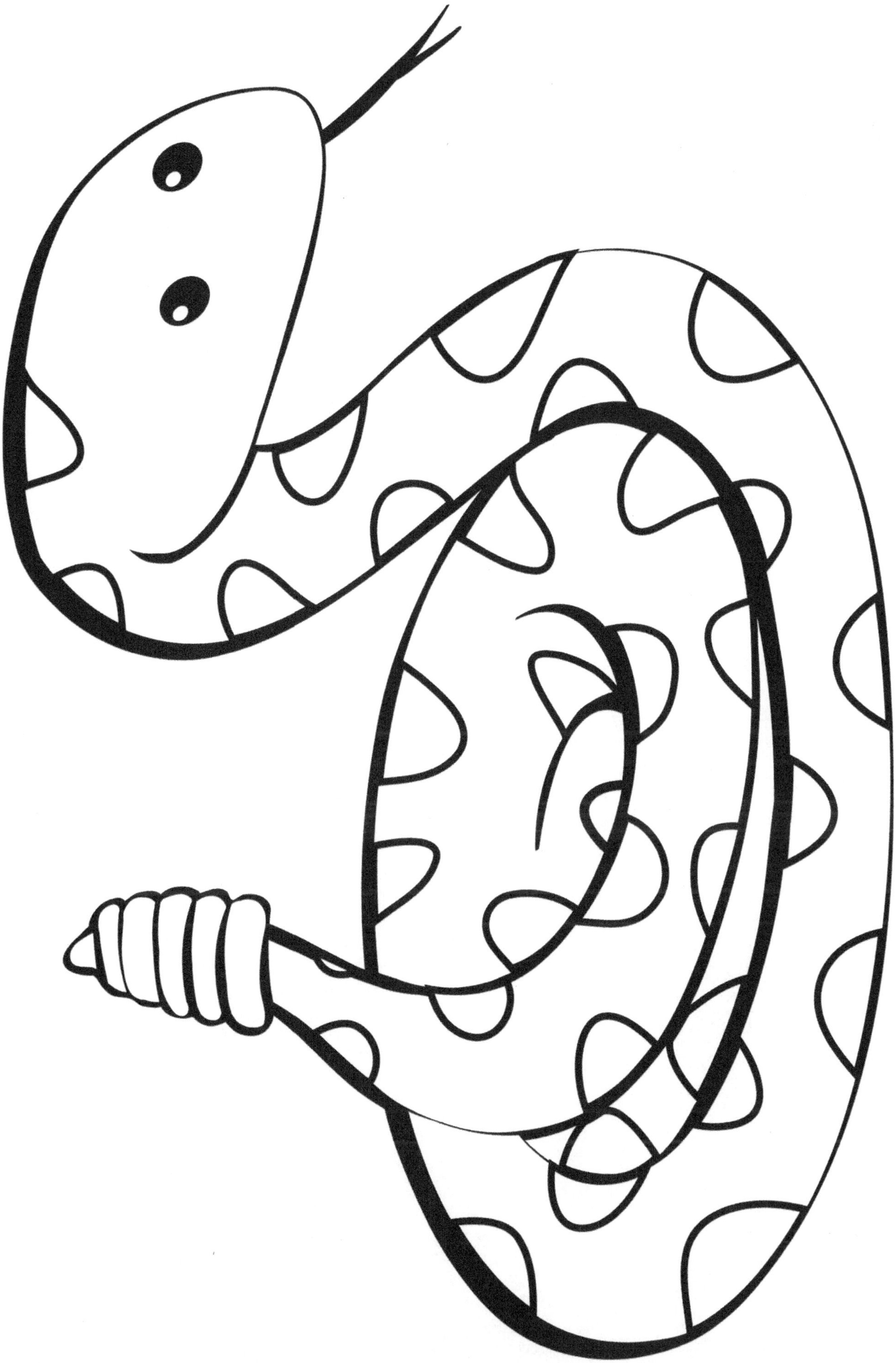

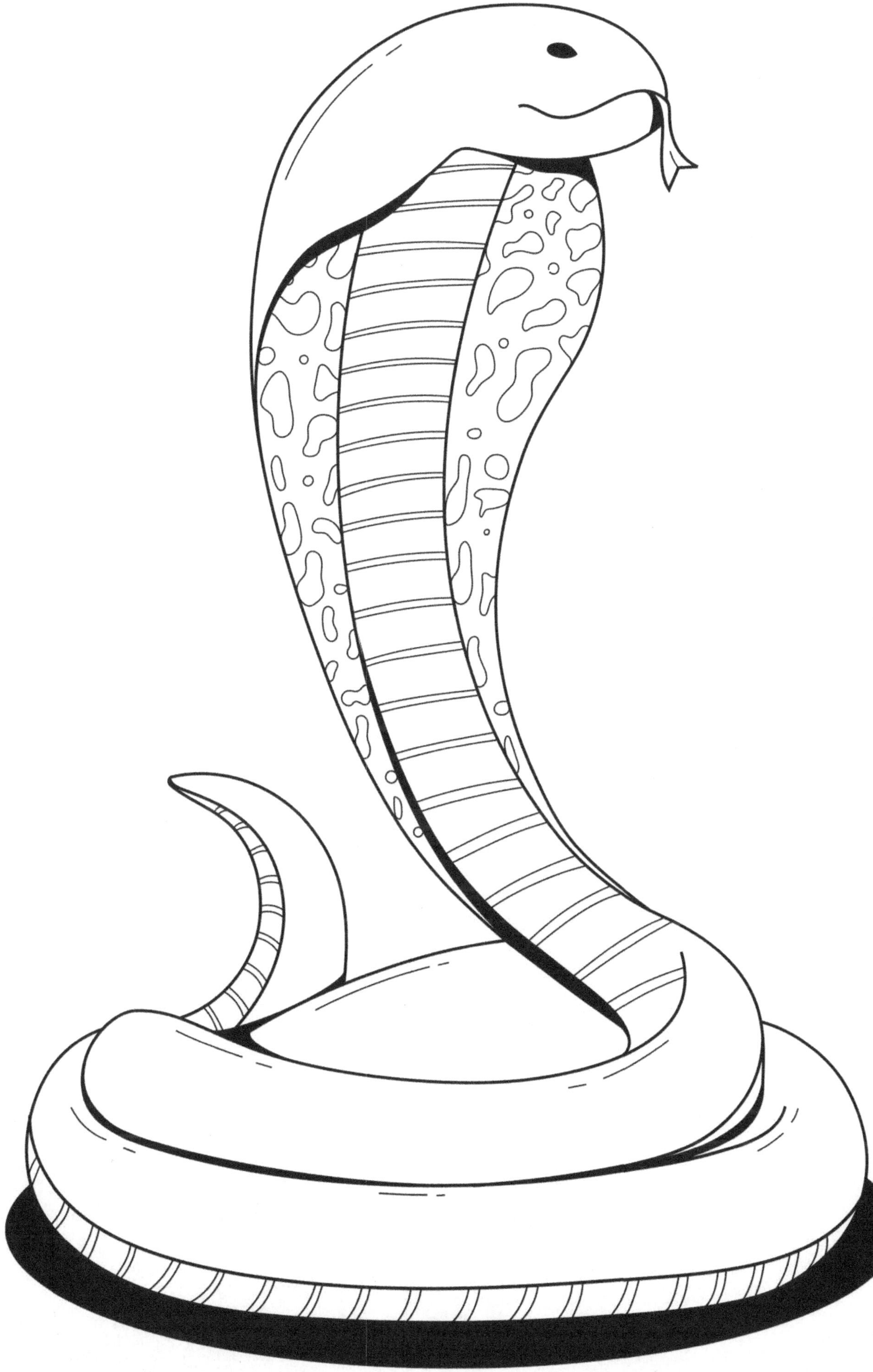

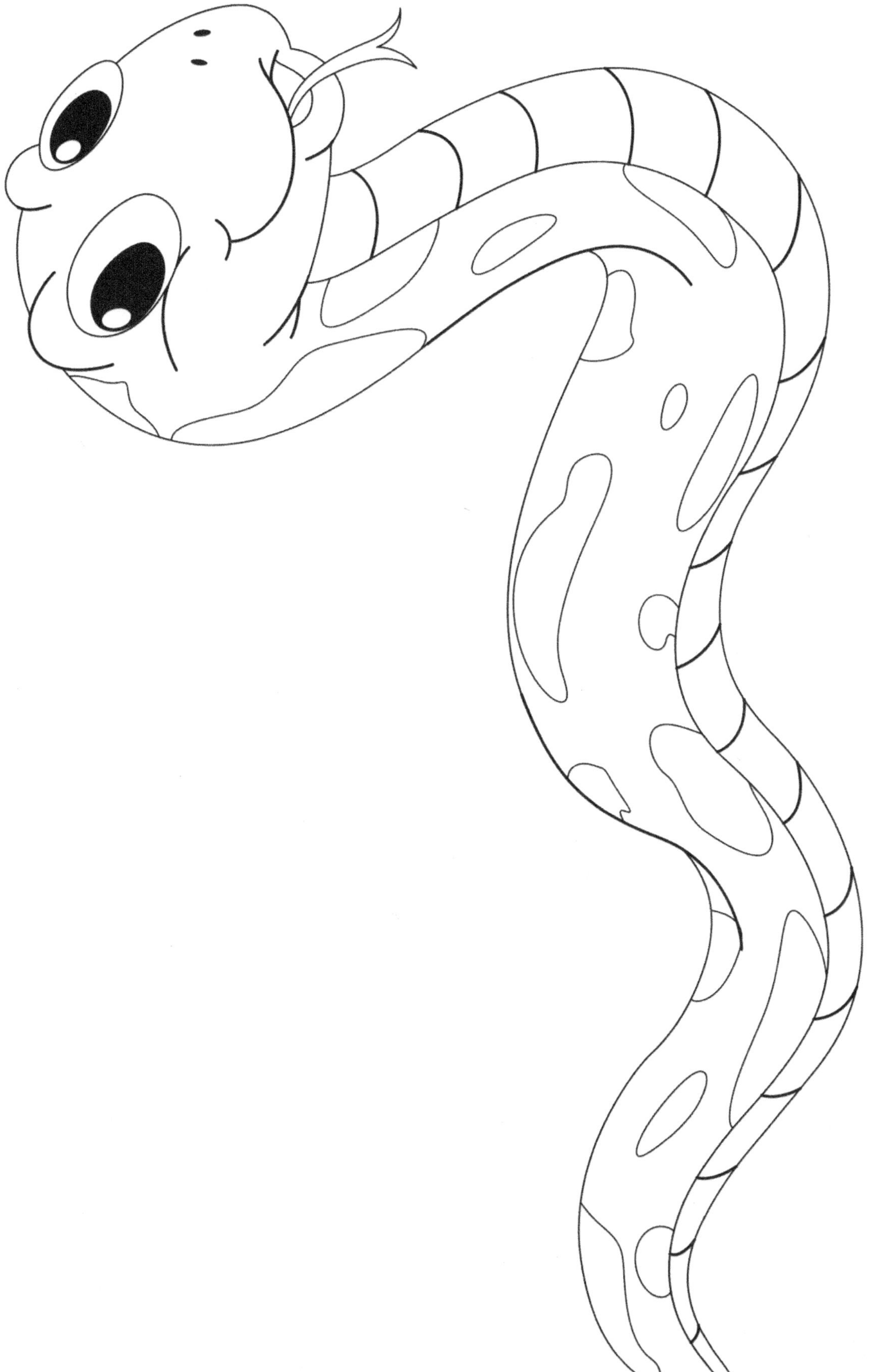

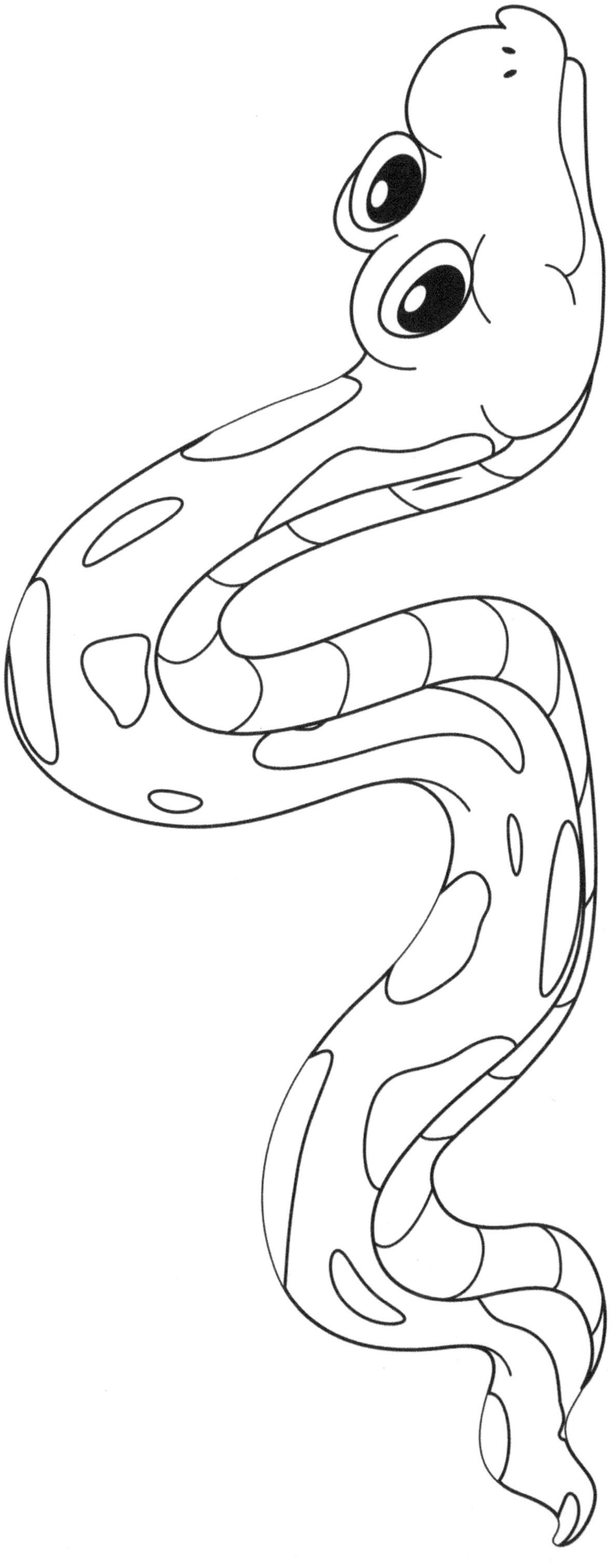

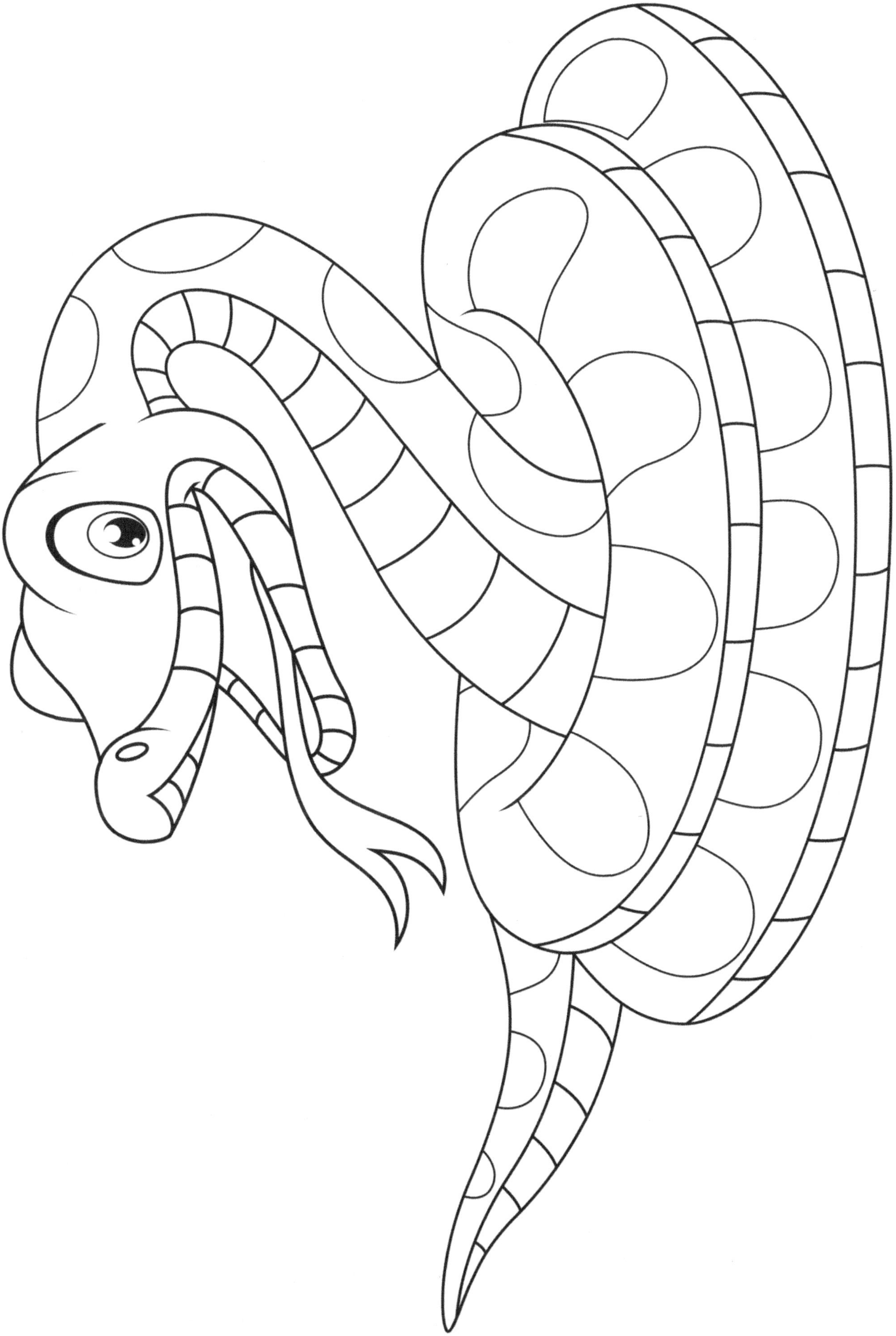

Made in the USA
Las Vegas, NV
10 December 2024

13774405R00033